T0158981

Jesus's
Royalty

PAULETTE LEWIS-BROWN

authorHOUSE®

AuthorHouse™
1663 Liberty Drive
Bloomington, IN 47403
www.authorhouse.com
Phone: 1 (800) 839-8640

Published by AuthorHouse 07/13/2018

ISBN: 978-1-5462-4373-1 (sc)
ISBN: 978-1-5462-4372-4 (e)

Contents

Who I Am

You Ask Me Who I Am
Well I Must Say This Loud And
Clear I Am Jesus Royalty.
Don't Put Me Last In The Line
Don't Throw Me First From
Your Heart.
Don't Make My Bed ☐ For Two.
Learn To Love Me From The Start.
Give Me Freedom To Breathe
This's Not A Botch Job.
If You Really Want To Know
Who I Am.
I Am A Child Of God.
Qualified To Be On First Page In This Book 📖
That's Who I Am.
Jesus Royalty From Birth.
Let the Truth cook.
Take a good Look.

The World Struggles

So Many People
Struggles With Faith
They Pray Daily
And Is Granted Grace.
The Devil Is On
The Side Line With His Plots
Jesus Steps In
With No Heart Attack.
The Devil Fights Back
With A Blood Clot Mode
To Hurt The Lungs.
A Family So Torn Apart,
No One Saw Death
Coming With A Code Blue.
Forgiveness At The Front Door
With King Jesus Truth.
The Devil Still Watching
From A Distance
Still Plotting To Tear
The Family Apart With A Stumble.
No Matter Which Side You're On.
The World Will Always
Struggle With The Truth.
Seek Jesus First.
Open The Front Door
And Let Him In.

Poetry Lines My Brain

While The World
Waits To See Change.
The Gifted Soul Rearranges
Every Aspect Of Life.
Using A Safety Net
To Catch Fishes.
Food For The Future
With No Ditches.
While The Word Is
Waiting For Change.
Change Is Not Waiting For You.
Follow Every Dream
With A Goal In Mind.
Only Jesus Change
Is Worth Anything For Clue.
It's Okay To Be Different
In Your Own Skin.
Climb The Mountain
And Win To Change.

While You Break My Heart

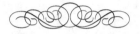

You Believe That You
Hold On To Something.
When In Fact Your Hurt
Didn't Worth A Thing.
It Couldn't Pay The Bills
Or Take Me To The Bank.
It Was Senseless It Almost
Cause A Heart Attack.
While You Break My Heart
And Still Out There
Looking For A Pay Day.
God Intervened And
Protect My Daily Bread.
Now I Am Living Peaceful
In The Arms Of My Husband.
The One That Was Created
For Me And My Vicinity.
Yes! A Jesus Punnaney Dis
Free from bondage and fear.

Holiness Freak

What If Your'e A Holiness Freak
Married Now With Nothing Underneath.
Not Everyone Will Be An Angel Under The Sheet.
Enjoy Every Moment With Your Partner.
Sin Is No Longer Creeping Under Your Window.
Passion Of Life Will Linger Forever.
Holiness Freak, Hallelujah. Jesus Property
Forever And Ever Amen.
Wait A Minute, Hallelujah All Over Again.
Thank You Jesus For My Best Friend.
Crazy Under The Sheet.

Jesus Loves Sinners Too.

Mr And Mrs Holy Moly
Stop Acting Like You're On
Top Of The World.
This Is Your First Clue
Jesus Loves Sinners Too.
Search Every Heart
Find True Love.
Give Every Soul Your Love
Ribbon. Dry Every Tears
With No Warning. This's Your
Second Clue, Jesus Loves
Sinners Too. Forgiveness Will
Always Welcome You.
Leave Every Burden At The Front
Door. Enter In With Your New Blue.
We Were All Sinners, And Yes!
Jesus Loves You. I Want A Ribbon Too.

Jesus Body

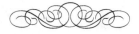

Mind, Body And Soul
All Jesus Property.
Where Your Thoughts
Enters Is A Zone To Carry You.
Balance Every Word
Like It's A New Shoe.
Beautiful But You Will
Never Get A Perfect Fit.
Wear And Tear Will Set
In On The Road To Success.
This's Jesus Body,
Balance Is Your Heart Beat To Rest.
Free Every Chamber
Of Hatred Fleas.
Jesus Body Only Sees Love.
From The Inside Out.
This Is Jesus Body
Come On, Lets Work It Out.
Work It Out, Work It Out.
Now, Share An Apple With Me.
Enjoy Jesus Body.

Don't Forget To Cry.

Don't Forget To Cry
Happy Tears.
When You're Happy.
You Know How To
Flood Your Space
When You Were Sad.
This Year Everyone Is
Going To Cry Happy Tears.
Don't Be Mad.
Create A Rainbow 🌈
And Embrace Promises. Smile
Today Embrace Every
Journey Like A Emphasis.
Don't Forget To Cry To
The Sound Of Jesus Loves You.
Give Me A High Five 🙌
And Say This I Know.
Guess Today's Gift 🎁.
This Poem Just Turns
Into A Happy Quiz😄.
Don't Forget To Cry For Joy.

Poetry World

Poetry In Every Pores
Suctioning My Brain
To Only Think Positive
Seeing A Light So Clear
Using Poetry To Regulate
Every Heart ♥ Rhythm.
Searching Every Soul
For The Perfect Piece
That Will Center Line My
Love For Poetry. Someday
A Poem For Everything Will
Be The Pie ☐ On This Day.
At Poetry World.
Feel Free To Own.
This Moment With Me.

Story On A Plate

Tell Me Your Story On A Plate.
Someday I Will Open A Gate
That Will Welcome You.
Your Struggles Was A Gift
From God. You Passed
With Flying Colors.
Someday Our Strength Will
Be The Highlight Of This Rainbow 🌈
And Stars ✦ Plate For
Conquerors
Tell Your Story On A Plate.
Bring Back Memories.

Without Peace

Without Peace
I Cannot Write.
Distraction Is Not
A Masterpiece. It's
A Stumbling Block
To Stop Success In
Its Track.
Without Peace You
Cannot Think For Two
Use Your Love To Find
Peace Within You.
This Poem Is Your First
Clue.
Prayer For Peace.

The Boat I Bought You.

The Boat □□ ♀ I Bought You Is
To Feed The Family Tree □.
Don't Forget To Share Your
Fishes 🐟 🐟 Even If
They're Already Frozen.
Invite Your Distance
Cousin Closer My Dear
The Boat □ I Bought
For You Is To Draw This Family
Closer With No Fear.
In The Future This Bond Will
Be Stronger, This's A Clue.
The Bought You. 🎁.

Only Jesus

Only Jesus Can Twist Me
No One Can Turn Me.
He's My Strength Forever
He Will Protect Me
Under His Wings.
Only Jesus Mercy Will
Carry Me On This Journey.
Create This Powerful T-Shirt.
Only Jesus Can Save You.
Wear This T-Shirt Again.

Jesus Punaany

Controversy Will Follow This Note
Only The True Jamaican Culture Will
Learn To Love Within Every Scope
Every Universal Soul, Sees Things
Differently, We're Still Bonded
In Our Culture And Decency.
However When Judgment Zones Steps
In Our Circle, We Will See Things From
A Broad Band Of Spectacles With Different
Rays. Punaany Is Jamaican Patois For The
Female Private Treasure, A Temple To Cherish
Forever. Jesus Property Is Another Version
Just One Way The World Wants To See It Cross
Over. Enjoy Every Culture With The Naked Truth.
Everyone Was Born Naked, With Love In Their Hearts.
Jesus Punaany Everywhere. For A Peace Of Mind
Just Dream On Jesus Property Instead. Now Pray And
Go To Bed.

Jesus Parade

Gather Every Happy Thoughts
Today You Will Express Yourself
Mold Together Every Broken Pieces.
Use This Flash Light To Put Them Together
Again. Look Beyond This Journey
Come Out Of The Stress Cave.
Let's Get Dress For Jesus Parade.
You're Not Less Than
You Are More Than Enough.
Here's A Sample,Take My Hand
Look At My Smile, Oh How Grand.
Two Of Us Are Ready For Jesus Parade.
Join With Me,Have No Fear.
Someday The World Will Welcome
Jesus Parade At Every Community Fair.
It's Okay To Look Different.

Innocent Prisoners

All Innocent Ones
Will Someday Be Free.
Jesus Is Working Hard
Behind Bars With Me.
To Create A
Vital Masterpiece.
Truth Will Open
\Every Cell Door.
Just Wait And See
A Lot More.
Innocent Prisoners Will
Walk This Freedom
Property. Lies Will Forever
Be Crippled By Their Own War.
The Innocent Prisoner
Will Forgive And Move On.
Let Jesus Shines Trough you.
Forgive The War.

Dance With Me

Dance 🕺 With Me
In This World Of
Poetry.
Stand By My Side
Don't Be An Enemy
Sing 🎵 With Me
You're Like My Family
The Core Of Every Heart
Should Be Love.
Dig Deep And Dance 🕺 With
Me. No Gloves ☐needed
Just Dance With Me Freely.

Brave Knows Your Name

Facing Challenges
Was A Nightmare
But You Pulled Through.
Life Journey Was Filled
With Lemons But You
Learn To Welcome Oranges
On The Same Tree.
You Endure Danger
And Pain Then Learn
To Skip Right Over
Another Challenge Again.
Bold Steps In To Hold
Your Hand. Your Heart Melts
When It Feels Like Bold And Brave
Now Become One .
What An Amazing Freedom
When Brave Knows Your Name.
Our Journey Could One Day
Feel The Same.
Prayer For The Brave Hearts
Will Forever Be On First Base.

Did You Write Me Off

Why Did You Write Me Off
Was I A Bad Debt On
Your Balance Sheet
Why Did You Write Me Off
Am I An Interference
In Your Inheritance Dream.
Why Did You Write Me Off
Today I Ask Myself This Question.
Someday We Will
Find The True Answer.
Did You Really Write Me Off
For No Apparent Reason.
Only God Knows.
Everything Is Jesus Property.
Please Don't Write Me Off.
Enjoy Jamaican Patois First
Just Before You Write Me Off.
See You In The Future.
I Will Be There Writing. ⚐Love Notes

Come For Your Gift.

Seriously
This's Not A Joke.
Come For Your Gift
It's Free From Jesus
Property Shift.
Come For Your Gift
Gear With Your Open
Mind And The Love That
You Share To Be Kind.
Always Be Prepared.
Come For Your Gift My Dear
Every Family Will Be
Rewarded, Some Sweet Day.
Spectacular Gift Give Away.
Right Now Just Come For
Your Gift I Pray.
Daily For Blessing.

Pour Down The Rain

If You're Down
On Your Luck,
Hold Your Peace.
Pray For Guidance
And A New Release.
Walk On
The Straight And Narrow.
Remember Everyone In The World
Have A Problem Shoe.
So Tell It All To Jesus
My Friend, This's True.
Watch Him Pour Down
The Rain Just For You Too.
Come On Dear Jesus
Pour Down The Rain.
Blessings For A New Shoe ⬩.
Show Me The Clue.
When You Pour Down The Rain.
Bless Me With Another Pair Of Shoes.

Mr Independent

Mr Independent
Gone Too Soon
I Am Sitting Here With
The Remote In My Hand
Watching Our Favorite Golf Station.
Thinking Of The Good Times
We Shared, Just Holding Hands.
Mr Independent I Remember
When You Were In A Band.
You Were The Center Piece
With Your Fun Sense Of Humor
That Attracts Everyone.
You Melt My Heart And Set
Me In A Happy Place.
Today This Chair Is Empty
Heaven Is Now Your New Home.
Mr Independent In My Heart
You're Never Gone.
Forever Loved By All.

My Old Pipe

My Old Pipe Knows History
My Old Pipe Knows Fame.
My Old Pipe Knows Mysteries
And Cartoon Names.
My Old Pipe Used To
Cut Sugar Cane In Jamaica
My Old Pipe Knows
Boundaries In America
My Old Pipe Travel
Every Where I Go.
Now I Am Resting In Peace
My Old Pipe Is Next To Me.
Stop Smoking In Fine Line.
A Note  From My Old Pipe.
Bugs Bunny Time,
The Name Of My Old Pipe.
Smile, This One Is For Free.
Go Ahead And Watch Your Tv ▬.
Stop Smoking Cancers Loves No Body.

Your Mission

Your Mission On Earth Will Be Hard.
Still Tackle And Win.
Stay In The Realms Of Your
Heart. Know Your Comfort
Quarter Rhythm.
Never Leave Yourself Wide Open.
Your Soul Is Also An Open Book.
Safety First Should Be The First Chapter.
Read This Poem Over Again In The Future
See Where Your Mission
Is Fun And Laughter.
Only Your True Friends
Will Carry You On This Mission.

Mother Diamond ◈

Mother Diamond
You Were My Strength.
Your Loyalty Will Live
On Forever.
Mother Diamond You
Were My Wealth.
Trusting In Each Other.
Mother Diamond Someday
We Will See Each Other Again.
Then The World Will
Comprehend That A Mothers
Love Is Like A Diamond, To
Share With Faith, Family And Friends.
Oh God Bless All Mother Diamond To The End.

Plant My Love.

Plant My Love.
Reap Kisses
Plant My Ability
Expect Crop For More Than Two.
Smile And Enjoy This
Facility Wishes.
Plant My Jokes
Reap A Peace Of Mind
Relax And Embrace My
Ever So Kind.
Plant This Journey
Enjoy Luxury
No One Saw Coming.
Now Send In The Stones.
One ♪ Way To Plant My Love.
Try Meditation.
For Comfort and Peace.

I Trust You

I Really Trust You
At The Same Level
That You Trust Me.
Don't Try To Pick
My Brain ☐ With Your
False Complaints Degrees.
Instead Trust Yourself
Enough To Only Tell The Truth.
Take A Deep Breath And
I Will Repeat After You.
I Trust Me At The Same
Level That I Trust You.
Now Put On Your Dancing Shoe.
This's The World First Clue.
Everyone Will Know What To Do.
If I Trust You.

To All Mothers

To All The Mothers
In The World □
Never Give Up Hope.
Your Job Will Be The
Hardest To Cope.
But Love And Loyalty
Will Steer You In The Face.
A Mothers Heart Is Filled
With Good Grace.
Peace And Love To Every
Mother On Earth.
Uplift Our Children
In Their Quest To Find The
Core Of Happiness.
Father God
Bless Every Mothers Love.
Forever Bonded.

Every Material Things.

Every Material Things
Belongs To The Creator
Of The Universe.
Enjoy Life To The Fullest
Leave Everyone With
A Mind Of Their Own.
Love Without Boundaries
Always Give On The Go.
The House
The Cars
The Yacht
The Bars
The Planes ✈
The Lands
The Trees
The Birds
The Jobs
All Belongs To The Creator
Of The Universe.
His Name Is Jesus.
All His Property.
Learn To Love
Freely.
This's Guardian One Angel Note.

Don't Run Away

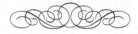

Don't Run Away
From Your Problems.
Stand In Your Faith
And Face Them.
Only One God
Control The Nation.
Don't Run
From Your Problems.
Only He Alone
Can Solve Them.
Balance Your Mind
Body And Soul.
Give Your Heart
This Plug To Hold.
Float If You Cannot Swim
Your Faith Will Draw You
Closer To Him.
Whatever Life Throws You.
Never Run
From Your Problems My Dear.
Select A Color From
The Rainbow
Now This's For You.
I Have The Same Color Too.
Don't Run Away
From Your Problems.
Have No Fear.
Uplift Your Faith
Daily In Prayer.
Say Amen.

Creative Goddess

Set This Stage To Be The Best.
Be Creative Is A Mindset
Deep In Your Thoughts
Is Your Magnet.
Draw Me Closer To You
Free Your Mind Of A Contest.
You're A Winner In This Sparkling ✦ Shoe.
Now Send Out Waves
You Are The Best.
Mr And Mrs Creative Goddess.
Smile For The World ☐
To See.
This poem is freedom.

Golden Eye

Expand Your Art
Create A Golden Eye
Believe In Yourself
Never Will You Lie
But Deep In Your Soul
You Can Create
A Third Eye Scary Cry.
Golden Eye With A Silver Brow.
Use Every Color Of The Rainbow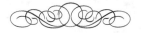
In The Background.
Your Gift Is All That You Know.
 Don't Feel Like A Clown
Peace ✌ Forever More To You.
No Need For A Frown Today.
Your Color Is Not Blue.

Step Of Faith

Step Out In Your Faith Dress.
Pray And Ask God For Forgiveness.
No One On Earth Is Perfect
So Climb The Ladder Of Success.
Just Remember The Breeze
Especially If You're Not Wearing
Anything Underneath.
Go Ahead This's Your Step Of Faith.
Use Hope To Uplift All The Courage In You.
Step Of Faith Is Your First Clue.
You Look Very Nice In Blue.
Here Is Your First Gift.
Come And Get It.
Your Free Will Blessings.
Will Repeat Itself
All Over Again

Happy Birthday

Set Everything In Motion
Only Happy Thoughts
On This Day.
Yes We Have A Voice So
Powerful On Our Birthday.
Every Heart Cry Out For Joy.
Show All The Gifts
And Wrap The Toys.
Bring Out The Girls And Boys.
Lavish True Love
Dance In The Moment
Feel Free On This Day.
Faith
Family
Friends
Will Sing Happy Birthday.
Yay!!.
Smile The Night Away.
Give Free Hugs Away

Look At That Smile

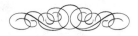

Look 👀
Look 👀
Look 👀
At That Smile.
Sparkling Eyes 👀
Oh So Wild 😀
Creative Minds
Are Now In Effect
See Where The Wise
Can Live On Suspense
Look 👀
Look 👀
Look 👀
At This Smile 😊
One 🔔 Note 📝
Will Be Yours To
Unwind.
The First Visible
Smile 😊 Will Be
The Winner Of This
Gift 🎁.
Look 👀
Look 👀
I Have To Be Quick.
You Have A Smile
That Will Light 💡
Up The Universe.
Yes!! Look 👀 At That
Smile ☐.
Beautiful.
Love Will Last
For A Life Time

Lies Fighting The Truth.

A Bag 💼 Of Lies
Sets In.
The Holy Truth
Creates Waves
From Within.
A Turmoil Of Lies
Swim Insight
The Naked Truth
Floats Your Way.
A Glove ☐ Of Lies
Knocks You Out.
Now Its Time
For The World To Pray.
Forgive Every Liar
Who Challenge The Truth.
Have Mercy
On Them Oh Lord.
Get Them Up
From Off The Floor.
Now Let's Eat.
This Is Not
A Challenge At All
Stay Away
From Liars Brawl.

Positive Soup Dish

Mix Up All Your Thoughts ☐ Today.
Happy Ones Are Like Lightening. Yay!!
Charge Your Heart
Then Set Things In Motion
Happy Birthday Is Top On The List.
Appreciation Is Not A Blood Test.
Gratitude 🔒 Is Your Greatest Ingredient.
Love Will Mixed It All In.
A Dash Of Seasoning Is
Your Choice. When You Eat
Always Be Nice 👍 ☐.
Smile With This Poetry Dish.
It's Your First Test.
Yes,Enjoy Your Birthday Gift.
Compliment From My
Positive Soup Dish 🍜.

It A Go Mad Them ♪

It A Go Mad Them
It A Go Drive Them Crazy
Wait Until They Can Read
Jesus Property.
Don't Keep The Innocent
One Down.
Don't Always Laugh
At A Funny Clown □.
Learn To See This World □
As A Merry Go Round.
Enjoy This Time Around.
Next Time We Will Be Laughing Together
On The Ground.
Get Up You Silly One ♪
It A Go Mad Them When
When They Can Read
And See Jesus Daily Plan For Us.
No More Catching The Bus 🚌.

Best Apple Pie Gift

Kiss Me Goodnight
But First Thing First
I Want Me Some Of Your
Delicious Apple Pie For Dessert
Send My Mind In A Frenzy
Best Apple Pie With
Ice Cream On Top.
Love With No Limits.
One Apple Pie At Arms Reach.
Free Anytime For This
Group To Eat.
Bless You.
Then Kiss Me Goodnight.
Make Belief.

Tell Me What Heaven Is Like.

Go Ahead Jesus Is Calling You Home
Visit Me In My Dreams.
Missing You Will Be On My Sleeve
Crying Tears Of Joy Is My Pain Key
Hugging Your Teddy Bear Is My Gear
No Replacement Is My Zone Of Comfort
Someday I Will Take A Hike
Tell Me What Heaven Is Like.
Is Jesus Hair Long Or Short
Is He Black Or White
Is He Slim Or Does He Have A Fat
Stomach Or A Bling, Bling.
Smile At My Silly Jokes.
I Am Sitting On This Bike
Tell Me What Heaven Is Like.
Rip My Love.
Send In A White Dove
To Pick My Brain.
Stop Me From Going Insane
Oh, I Am Missing You.
Give Me A Call Tonight
Tell Me What Heaven Is Like...
Earth Feels Like Hell
Without You My Love.

Be The Best You Can

Educate Yourself
Research If Your'e Not Sure.
Feel Free To Speak Out.
Your Opinion Matters
Don't Be Afraid To Help Others
Open Your Heart In The Sharing
Department.
Never Forget To Feed Yourself.
Be The Best In Your Field.
It's Okay If You Fall In The Second Best
Category, Do Not Worry.
Work Harder Next Time.
Practice Will Get You Close Enough To
Almost Perfect. Trust Your Gut Feelings
Create A Fan. Someday You Will Be The Best
Candidate To Regulate Every Heart Rhythm.
Be The Best That You Can.

Pray Daily

What If Everyone Pray Daily
Would This World Be A Better Place?
Would We Feel Lighter
Without Sin Or Disgrace.
What If Forgiveness
Came To Us First?
Would Our Prayer
Just Wash All Bad Thoughts
Away Forever?
What If We Go Down On Our Knees
And Humbly Ask God For Forgiveness.
Could You Get Up In That Tight Dress?
Smile With Your Good Sense Of Humor.
Use It As A Reminder
To Pray Daily.
Hallelujah
Amen.

Don't Struggle With Love.

Love Allows Your Blood
To Flow Freely,
Not With Sympathy.
No Restriction Or Blood Clot.
True Love Doesn't Hurt.
Your Brain Is In Accordance
With Your Balance.
Jumpstart Your Life With
A Fresh Outlook At Love.
Free Your Mind From
Toxic Relationships
Breathe In Clean O2.
Cast Out Negativity, For Truth.
The Main Reason Is.
Don't Struggle With Love.
Seek Advice From The Creator Up Above.
Heal Your Heart.
Don't Struggle With Love.
Love Knows No Boundaries.

Can't Stop Progress

Your Gossip Can't Stop Me
Your Doubt Can't Stop Me
Your Selfish Point Of View
Can't Stop Me
Your Ability To Put Me Down.
Can't Stop Me.
There's No Need To Call Stress.
You Can't Stop My Progress.
Enjoy Your Life And Be Blessed.
Nice 👍☐ Dress 👗.
Welcome Success

Rich Or Poor

Rich Or Poor
Come On Over.
Enjoy This Luxury Sofa.
Everything Is Jesus Property.
Feel At Home Under Your
New Roof.
Make Yourself At Home
Family Is An Open Heart
That's Willing To Share And Expect
Nothing In Return My Dear.
Rich Or Poor Come Under This Umbrella.
Let's Eat And Feed The World ☐ Forever.

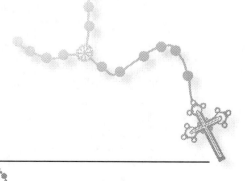

Be Goofy

Be Goofy
Be Silly
Be Anything
You Want To Be.
Step Out Of Your Body
Be Someone Else
Be Oprah Winfrey
Without Money
Be Bob Marley Without
Reggae Music.
Be Goofy Again
Now Call All Your Friends.
See How Fast All Of Them
Took Sick.
Then They Call And Ask If
You're Homeless.
This Was Just A Test.
Be Goofy Again This Time Be The Best.
No Need To Call Fake Friends.
Goofy.
Goofy.
Be Bless.

The Color Of The Rainbow

I Feel Like I Belong
When I See The Color
Of The Rainbow
This Beautiful Promise
That I Will Never Be Alone.
I Feel So Strong
When It Rains.
True Blessings From Above.
No More Flood.
Yes!!
Just Enjoy This
Beautiful Rainbow
With Everyone.
Rest Assure I Will Be In Heaven
Smiling Down
Enjoy Every Color Of The Rainbow.
Find Peace Within,
From Your Dear Friend Glenn.

Lighthouse Blues

Navigate Yourself To Me
Find Me In The Lighthouse
Up On The Hill.
Look Out For My
Light Will Be
Shining Bright.
No More Fake Promises
Just Real
Courage And A Trust
Factor Refill.
Cover Me With Your
Strong Muscle Tone.
Kiss Me Goodnight.
Hold Me Close
Until I Melt In Your Arms.
Smile And Enjoy
This Lighthouse Blues.
Look Around For Real
Seductive Clues♥.

A Caregivers Dream

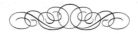

Organize The Most Spectacular
Event Of Your Lifetime.
Golden Palm Tree
Is Your Theme For Free.
Invite Everyone In Your Circle.
Don't Leave Out Their Families,
Who Are Broken.
Open Your Heart ♥
For A Moment,
And Then Breathe
Donate 50% To Alzheimer's Disease.
This's Every Caregiver Dream.
And This's One 🕯 Angel 😇 Note 🖼.
Say Hello 👋MARY.
Quote:
Healing For Alzheimer's Disease
Is In The Making.
Poetry Is The Stem
Regulate Every Heart Rhythm,
Then View The Root
Of The Brain 🧠
Enjoy The Creative Dream

To Every Gifted Soul.

To Every Gifted Souls
In The Universe.
Your'e Different
For A Reason.
Go Feed That To
The Birds Mentality
Cannot Challenge You.
No What Goes Up
Must Comes Down
Side Remarks
Will Not Affect You.
Stay Focus With Your
Creative Mindset.
Someday Everyone Will Own
A Poetry Pillow
To Cry 😣 On.
One 🎵 Love To Every
Gifted Souls.
Moonwalk To This One 🎵.
Who Did You Think Of?
Yes, He Was Gifted Too.

Meow  Meow

Meow
Meow
Where Is The Kitty Cat?
With The Show Me How.
Meow
Meow
Where Is Maddy, Hazel And Minnie.
Meow
Meow
Why Are They Calling You The Cat Lady Jackie.
Meow
Meow
Express Yourself With Bravery. Be Witty Not Sniffy
Love All Your Cats Friends
Welcome Everyone Cat Business □
Our Cat Name Is Casey Love Nest.
Meow
Meow.
Kitty Kitty Free Free.☺
Say Out Loud Under This Oak Tree.
Meow
Meow.
A Wild Cat For Everyone
One Juicy Plan.
Meow.
You're The Best Glamour
Glam.
Meow
Meow.

Wuff, Wuff

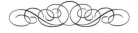

Where Are The Dog Lovers?
Wave 👋 □ So I Can See Your Paws.
Wuff
Wuff
Thwirl For This Cause.
Show Me You're Latest Threats
For Our Furry Friends.
Their Loyalty Will Live
With Us To The End.
Wuff
Wuff
Make It Rain □ On This Day Lord.
Shower Us With Doggy Blessings.
True Love ❤ Forever.
Humanity Love Sets In.
Remembering Our Doggy Friends.
Wuff
Wuff

Mr And Mrs Compassionate

Send In Mr And Mrs Compassionate.
Genuinely Caring For Others.
Grace Is Theirs To Give.
Their Faith Is The Strongest
A Gift So Powerful,
No Man Can Break.
Mr And Mrs Compassionate ♥
Will Give Or Take.
Uplift In Prayer Is A Keepsake.
Genuinely Blessed With
Their Love For Others.
Send In Mr And Mrs Compassionate Again.
We Are Celebrating Everyone
In This Room Today.
Smile,
I Can Read Your Eyes.
Mr Compassionate For Life.

Serious Business Idea

This Thought Flashes
Through Your Mind.
Taking Center Piece And
In High Gear.
Everyone In Sight Is Waiting
For The Punch Line
So Many Will Have A Real
Point Of View.
See Where Yours Matters
Plug This Poem As A Guessing Factor.
Smile With A New Business Idea.
Select A Winner With So Little Clues.
My Idea Stands Out Brighter In The Crowd.
This Art Will Stands
Out Loud in
A Serious Business Idea.

Creative Tea Party

Dress Like Royalty
Prim And Proper
Your Colors Will
Stand Out In Many Numbers
Hats From Every
Walks Of Life.
Do Not Forget The Color Purple
Everyone Looks Pretty Smart
Leave Room For A Special Girdle
Five Inches Off Base Okay.
Smile And Enjoy
This Beautiful Day
Filled With Fun
And Good Play.
Snacks Galore,
Dancing Sandwiches
Calling My Name.
Eat Me Please
This Is My Way Of Sharing
A Creative Tea Party
Beautiful Women Eating In Style.
Etiquette Please.
Where's Is The Laughter
Later I Need A Tea To Go.
Oh How Creative.
Take This Hat To Go.

Royalty Angel

Writing ✍ At 0400am
Begging Father God For
Mercy. Grace And Hope
In Clear Sight. This Royalty
Poem Feels So Humanly Right.
Royalty Angel Is Only A
Dream. Long Live The Not
So Perfect One.
The Rest Of The World Will Someday Carry
On. This Not So Perfect Poem.
Royalty Angels Smiling From Heaven.
Perfection Still Belongs To Jesus.
Amen 🙏.

Celebrate This Special Moment

Give Freely
Your Heart ♥ Is
An Open Book.
Think Of Me
When You Need
A Recipe From A
Good Cook 👤⊙
Look Around Selct
Your First Celebration
For Today. Ask The Most
Important Question.
Is Today Your Birthday 🎂
Celebrate This Happy Moment
My Way.
Happy Birthday 🎁.
Here's Gift To Share
The Kitchen With you

My Hope

My Hope Is For Everyone
To Make It To Heaven.
Having This Party
All Over Again
With Jesus Angels.
Everything Is Free.
What If I Serve Jesus
His Coffee ☕ Black.
Smile My Dear,
There Will Be
No More Heart Attack.
No Pain Or Sorrow
Just Clean Bill Of Health.
What Story Could I Share With Jesus
When He Already Knows Everything.
Heaven Is Going To Be Beautiful.
My Hope Is To See Everyone.
Wearing Their Faith
Be Strong Dress 👗.
I Know What You're Thinking.
All The Men Will Be Naked.
Free From Sin.
Hope Comes A Long Way
To Heaven 👼. This's A New
Beginning For Jesus Angels.
My Hope Lives On Forever.

Powerful Note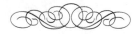

You Have Come A Long Way.
This's Your Rainy Day
Enjoy Your Gifted Blessings.
Someday Get In A Row And
Enjoy The Rainbow
Every Beautiful Color
Stems From The Walls Of Heaven.
Time To Vote
Show Me Your Powerful Note.
Everyone Is A Winner See My
Powerful Quote.
Call Out For Mary
Then Read My Powerful Note.
Have Fun.
See You Tomorrow.
Spread Your Wings.

Always Smile

Always Smile
It Doesn't Matter What.
Never Cloud ☁ Your Smile
With Your Thoughts Of
Grey. Just Live Your
Happiness Your Way.
Your Smile Is Your Center
Piece. A Beautiful Light In
The Distance Is Waiting To
See You Smile.
Smile Will Open Your Heart
Forever To See Only Love.
Embrace Life, Always Smile
When You See A White Dove
Just Go Ahead And Smile
Free Your Mind:
And Live.

Hope And Grace

Hope And Grace
Builds A Wall.
They Invited Faith
To Uplift This Thought.
Then Walked In Peace And Love.
With Prayer Standing By.
Perseverance And Patience
Checking In On Time.
Just To See How We Unwind.
Happiness Is Peeping
From Behind This Wall.
Not Everyone
Will Understand This Call.
Brave Stand Up
In The Crowd And Say.
Hope And Grace Be Strong.
You're Creating
A Genius Invisible Wall.
Just Throw In The Rain ☐
Sun ☀ Moon ☽ And Stars ✦
We Will Need The Tree ☐
To Cover This Note.
Rainbow ☁ Promises.
This Wall Is Forever.
It's Okay To Cry Too.
Tears Of Joy Is All Over This Wall.
Church Bells Ringing With
Father, Son And Holy Spirit.

Paid In Full

All Your Bills
Will Be Paid In Full One Day.
No Need To Doubt God
He Always Have Your Back.
Just Pray.
Wellness Centers
Will Know Your Name.
No More Heart Attack.
No Way.
Paid In Full Will Be A Project.
Trust God In Everything
You Do.
Make This A Habit.
Hello Jackie, Show Me A Bill
Jesus Wants It To Be Paid In Full.
Be Happy For The Future

Money Is A Tree

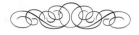

Money Is A Tree
Plant It And Watch It Grow.
Feed The Root
Remember The Branches
Watch Money Grow
Because Someday
It's Going To Grow On Trees.
Next Time You Read This Poem
Show Me Your Money Tree.
Name Your Special Tree.
Peace Clear My Lungs.

Diddly Diddly Boo

Diddly
Diddly
Boo.
Gifts  Are
Wrapped Up In
This Clue.
Wave ✋☐ Your Hands
To See Who Can
Spare You A
Diddly
Diddly
Boo
Scary Miss Lue
Singing Diddly
Diddly Boo 👻
What's The Name
Of This Avenue
Boo.
Jamaica Is The
First Clue.
One Love.
Diddly
Diddly
Boo.
Scary World Will Do
The Diddy Diddy Boo.

Father God Loves You

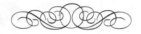

Father God Loves You
Never Doubt His Will
Enjoy Every Moment
You're One Of His
Masterpiece.
Give Freely
From The Heart
Love Yourself First.
It's Okay To Uplift Others,
Still Find Time
To Uplift Yourself.
Father God Loves You.
He's My Father Too.
Glory
Glory 🙈.
Lives On This Avenue.

World Royalty Poem

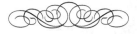

Scope The Surface
Everyone Looks Beautiful
Look For The Exit Signs 📖
Everyone Knows The Entrance.
Because We're In.
Lay Down Your Safety Mat
Welcome All In This Palace Hut.
Prayer 🙏 First.
No Mask 😷 Will Be Needed
Freedom From Sin Lives Within.
Be Bold And Beautiful
When You Think Of Me.
This Poem Is Given To
Every Angel On Earth
Royalty Grows
From The Heart.
Smile And Enjoy This Journey.
Royalty.

Show Me Wisdom

Father God
Show Me Wisdom
Teach The World
Please Show It To Me.
I Want To See
The Wise Man Mirror.
Will It Exclude Me.
Will I See The Need
Before The Wants.
Will I See The Inner Strength
Or Will I Look
From The Surface.
Show Me Wisdom
Your Number One
Favor To Me.
Dear God Give Me
Wisdom And Peace.
Start From Within.

Write For The World

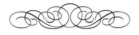

Write For The World
Do Not Spend
Your Focus On One 🔔.
Everyone Will Need
A Blessing Someday
Your Gift Will Feed A Nation
Write For The
World Is Your Bond.
Keep Your Faith
As Center Piece.
Peace And Love
Will Closely Follow
Grace And Gratitude
In Clear View.
Write For The World.
Poetry Dessert 🔔
An After Meal Thought
Is Coming Through.
Write For The World
I Will Show You What To Do.
Wait You Next Gift
Is Coming Through.

Cactus 🌵 For Everyone

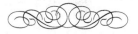

Give Everyone A Cactus 🌵
Let Freedom Reign
We Started Out Smooth
Then Change In The Rain ☐
We Grow With Our Rough
Edges. No One 🎵 Feels The
Same.
When Life Throws You Lemons
On A Sunny Day.
Smile In The Moment And Kiss 💋
Your Cactus. No Mayday.
Cactus 🌵 For Everyone.
I Will Always Be Near💛.
At The Nearest Point.
Prayer 🙏 Lives Within.
Oh So Clear
Kiss A Cactus Today

The World Economy

The World Economy
Is Far From Perfect.
Everyone Is On A Journey
Someday We Will Practice
What We Preach. Don't Look For
The Perfect Church 🔔
Economy Starts In Your Heart.
Keep It Clean.
Never Worry About Controversy.
Enjoy The Raindrops
Smile When You Can See Your
Blessings On Tippy Toes
Share With The Community
Gifts From Your Overflow
Spring From Your Heart
Starts In A Garden Of Love.
Reboot And Restart
The World Of Economy.

Make Me A Happy Fan

Make Me A Happy Fan
To Cool Things Down.
Send Me In The Glamour Glam
Let Everyone Know Your Name.
Poetry Is A New Invention
Put It On The World Daily Plan.
Make Me A Happy Fan
To Cool The Temperature
In This Blue Corner.
Mary And Jane Is Leaving
Way Too Soon.
Bright Up The Room
With Rainbow🌈 Colors For Everyone.
Take A Peek At My Happy Fan.
You Heard It Here First.
Happiness Is Not A Disease 😄.
So Embrace This Happy Fan Moment.
Fresh Cool Breeze
Feels Like Heaven.

Pitt Bull Dilemma

Stop Setting Up Pitt-Bulls
In A Close Knit Quarter.
Stop Before This Turn Into
A Project Disaster
Love All Animals Is
Good And Proper.
Know That Pitt-Bulls
Have Unpredicted Behavior.
Lesson Learn From
An Animal Lover.
Safety First
Is Your Number One Cover.
Prevention Is Your Code.
Protect Our People Who
Can No Longer See The Danger.
Creeping Under A Crisis Border
Called Pitt-Bull Dilemma.
No Need To Apply Pressure
Stop This Before It Happen.
No Room For Another Disaster.
No Need For A Pitt Bull Dilemma.

Smile In Every Moment

Smile In Every Moment
Life Is Not As Bad As We
Think.
Open Every Mindset And
Welcome A Wink ☺
No Need For Troubles And
Collapse Lungs Drama.
Smile In Every Moment
You're Still A Winner.
Shower This World With
Blessings Forever.
Welcome Everyone Even Sinners.
Smile In Every Moment Shocker.
Be A God Sent For Someone In Need.
Plant Your Seed Then Watch It
Grow Into Something Beautiful.
Smile In Every Moment.
Forever Loved By One.
This Coin Is Yours.

Peace And Love.

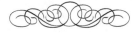

Peace And Love
Lives In Every
Household.
Find In The Heart
That Knows Only
Love.
Prayer 🔐 Will Travel
Along Way.
Daily Peace ✌ Comes
From Above.
Encourage Others
To Find Peace And Love
With Jesus On First Base.
One 🔔 Messenger Purpose
On Earth 🌏. Spending Time
With Peace And Love ❤.
This's Forever Happiness.

Legacy Of Love

We Live
We Learn
We Practice
What We Preach.
Everyone Was Born
Naked With Love In
Their Heart.For A Sheet.
Search Every Heart
Share This Poem Of
Hope. Legacy Of Love
A Shield Forever.
Learn How To Cope
In This World Forever.
Be A Legacy Of Love 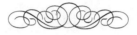.
We're Sisters And Brothers
Sheltering Under One
Umbrella. Sharing Legacy
Of Love.

I Live My Life

I Live My Life
In Many Colors
Just Like The Rainbow
I Traveled The World
Without Judgment.
I Learn To Let Things Go.
Finding Peace
Was Easy It Lives
Within Our Souls.
I Live My Life
With Jesus Saying,
My Child Be Bold.
I Was The Only Perfect One.
I Live My Life
To Please Him.
Everyday Is A Learning
Experience Anthem.
Embrace The Rainbow
To The End.
Enjoy Life With Faith,
Family And Friends.
Be True To Your Promises.
Live Your Life.

Walk The 5k For Alzheimer's

Dress The Path
This's For A Good Cause.
Give Back To This Community
Stay Focus, No Distraction Needed.
Walk This Path Before Event Day
Practice Over And Over Again.
Think Deep And You Will See The
Winning Prayer 🙏.
Smile At The End Of This Race.
Your Mentor John
Will Be In Clear Sight
Reviewing Your Pace.
Have Fun In Good Faith.
Everyone Will Celebrate
This Walk For
Alzheimer's Disease.
Heal Every Brain ☐ On This Hot,
Walking In A Circle Day.
Water Me Down With Your Smile.
I Really Don't Need
To See A Mayday,
On This Beautiful
Alzheimer Special Event.
Say Yes We Did It Again.
We're All Champions.
In This Alzheimer's race.

Love Basket

Share My Love Basket
Something For Everyone.
Like My Love Basket
Create A Way To
Start Your Own.
Faith Will Guide You
With Wisdom.
See Everything Beautiful
Then Fill Your Love
Basket With Love.
Holy Bread 🍞 Is Just
One Note 🎵.
Welcome This Love Basket
I Pray.
A Forever Quote.
Love Basket For The World.

The Bargain Box

This's My Gift To You
Make It Your Own.
Create A Masterpiece
On Top.
This Box Is Yours To Keep.
Welcome The World Filled
With Creative Moods And Needs.
Open Your Mind.
Everything Must Go Is
Your Daily Flow.
Balance This Journey
Circle O For The Right
Spot.
Create Your Own Bargain
Box 🎁.
Community Lavish in Love.
Smile And Welcome 👯
The Bargain Box.
Something For Everyone.

Jesus Help The Children

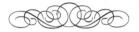

Jesus Help The Children
See Their Safety First
Provide Shelter And Food
For Them, And Only Love
To Share Around The Bend.
Protect Your Children
Daily Lord.
Wash Their Tiny Feet.
Prayer For Every Household
All Over Again.
Safety Under The Sheets.
Our children Are The Future.
Keep Them Safe Forevermore.
Open A World
Of Happiness At Every Door.

Printed in the United States
By Bookmasters